For Alina, Guillem, and their Grandpas!
Lots of love, Viv/Gran xxx

For Sam and Phil, with love
N.R.

First published 2025 by Walker Books Ltd 87, Vauxhall Walk, London SE11 5HJ

2 4 6 8 10 9 7 5 3 1

Text © 2025 Vivian French
Illustrations © 2025 Nanette Regan

The right of Vivian French and Nanette Regan to be identified as author and illustrator respectively
of this work has been asserted in accordance with the Copyright, Designs and Patents Act 1988.

EU Authorized Representative: HackettFlynn Ltd, 36 Cloch Choirneal, Balrothery,
Co. Dublin, K32 C942, Ireland. EU@walkerpublishinggroup.com

This book has been typeset in Stempel Garamond LT Std

Printed in China.

British Library Cataloguing in Publication Data:
a catalogue record for this book is available from the British Library

ISBN 978-1-5295-0848-2

www.walker.co.uk

MIX
Paper | Supporting
responsible forestry
FSC® C008047

WALKER BOOKS
AND SUBSIDIARIES
LONDON • BOSTON • SYDNEY • AUCKLAND

# CHICK, CHICK, CHICK, CHICK, CHICKEN!

VIVIAN FRENCH

NANETTE REGAN

When we stayed with Grandpa, it was sunny.
"It's too nice to stay indoors," Grandpa told us.
"Why don't we go and see the chickens?"
"Do I like chickens?" asked my brother Bob.
"I don't know," I said. "Let's go and see."

Grandpa led the way down the garden.
There was a fenced-off area and I pointed
to the little wooden house in the middle.
"Look, Bob!" I said. "That's the hen house.

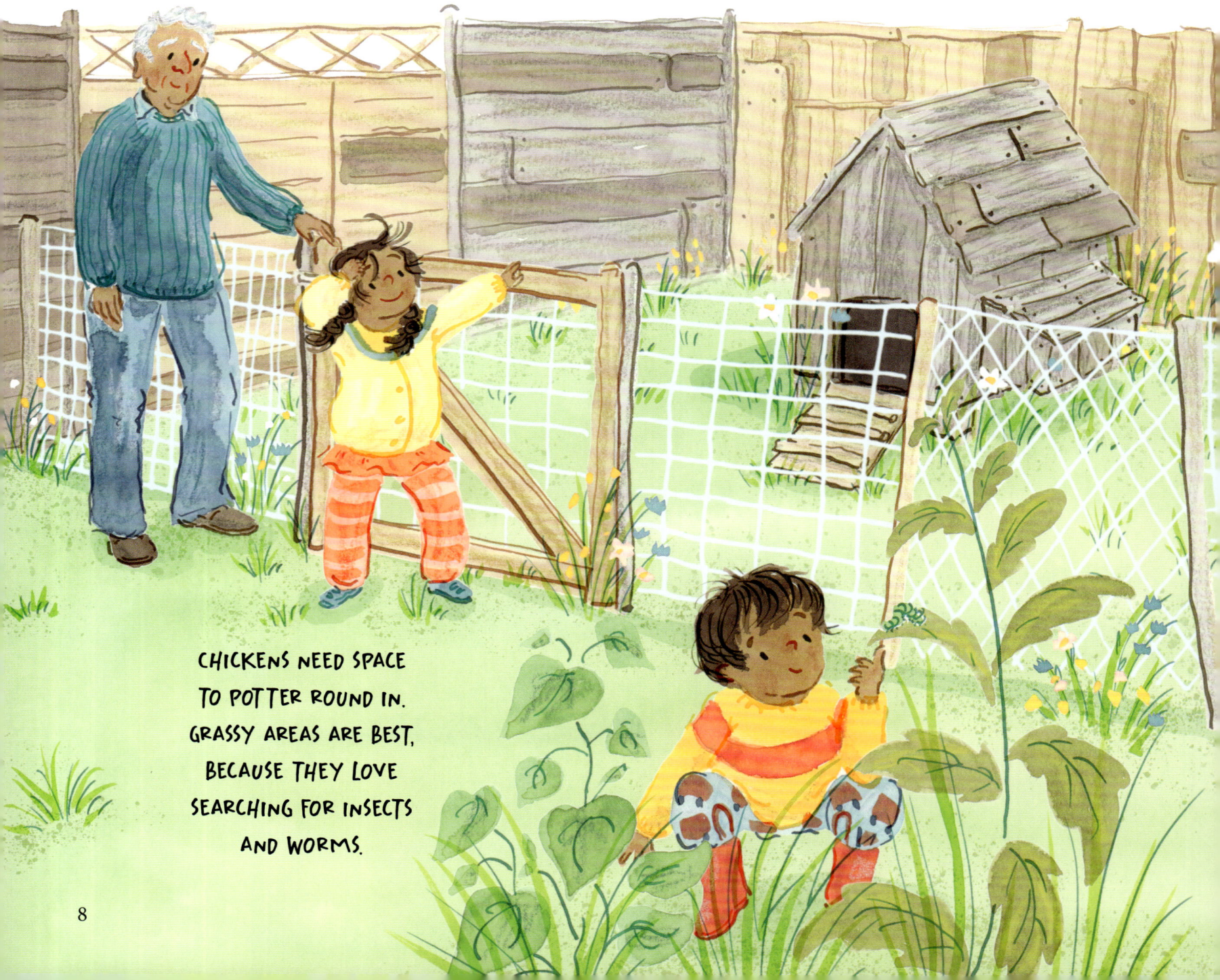

CHICKENS NEED SPACE
TO POTTER ROUND IN.
GRASSY AREAS ARE BEST,
BECAUSE THEY LOVE
SEARCHING FOR INSECTS
AND WORMS.

They've got perches to sleep on, and litter on the floor
to catch their droppings – and there's a nest box,
too, where they lay their eggs."

NEST BOX

PERCHES

LITTER

WATER

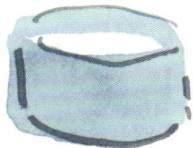

CHICKENS SHOULD ALWAYS HAVE LOTS OF
WATER AVAILABLE TO DRINK.

A chicken came bustling out: its feathers were white and silvery, with black edges.

Then another: yellowy brown, with a red rubbery crest and beard.

THE CREST ON A CHICKEN'S HEAD IS CALLED A COMB, AND THE BEARD IS CALLED A WATTLE.

"The brown one's Lola. She's an Orpington chicken," Grandpa told Bob. "The other's Lulu. She's a Wyandotte."

ORPINGTON AND WYANDOTTE CHICKENS LAY AROUND 200 LARGE BROWN EGGS A YEAR.

Then came a sudden sound.
"What's that?" Bob jumped.
I laughed. "That's Marvin!
He thinks he's the boss."

COCK-A

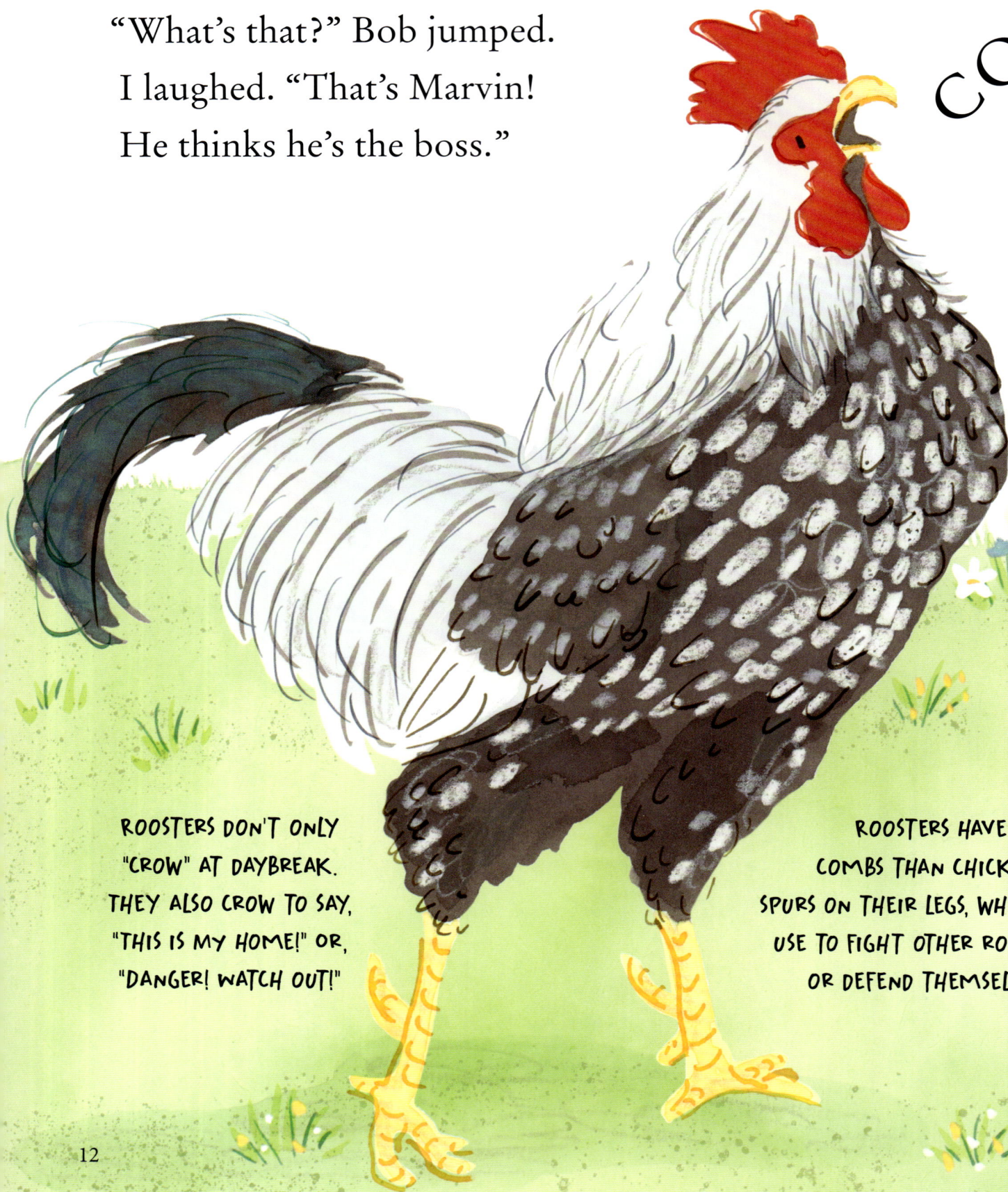

ROOSTERS DON'T ONLY
"CROW" AT DAYBREAK.
THEY ALSO CROW TO SAY,
"THIS IS MY HOME!" OR,
"DANGER! WATCH OUT!"

ROOSTERS HAVE BIGGER
COMBS THAN CHICKENS AND
SPURS ON THEIR LEGS, WHICH THEY
USE TO FIGHT OTHER ROOSTERS,
OR DEFEND THEMSELVES.

-DOODLE-DOO!

Marvin came strutting over.
"You can tell he's the rooster,"
said Grandpa. "See his splendid tail feathers?"

Grandpa tossed some grain.
"Watch what he does now."
Lulu and Lola rushed over,
but Marvin stayed put.
"He makes sure the others
get enough first," I told Bob.

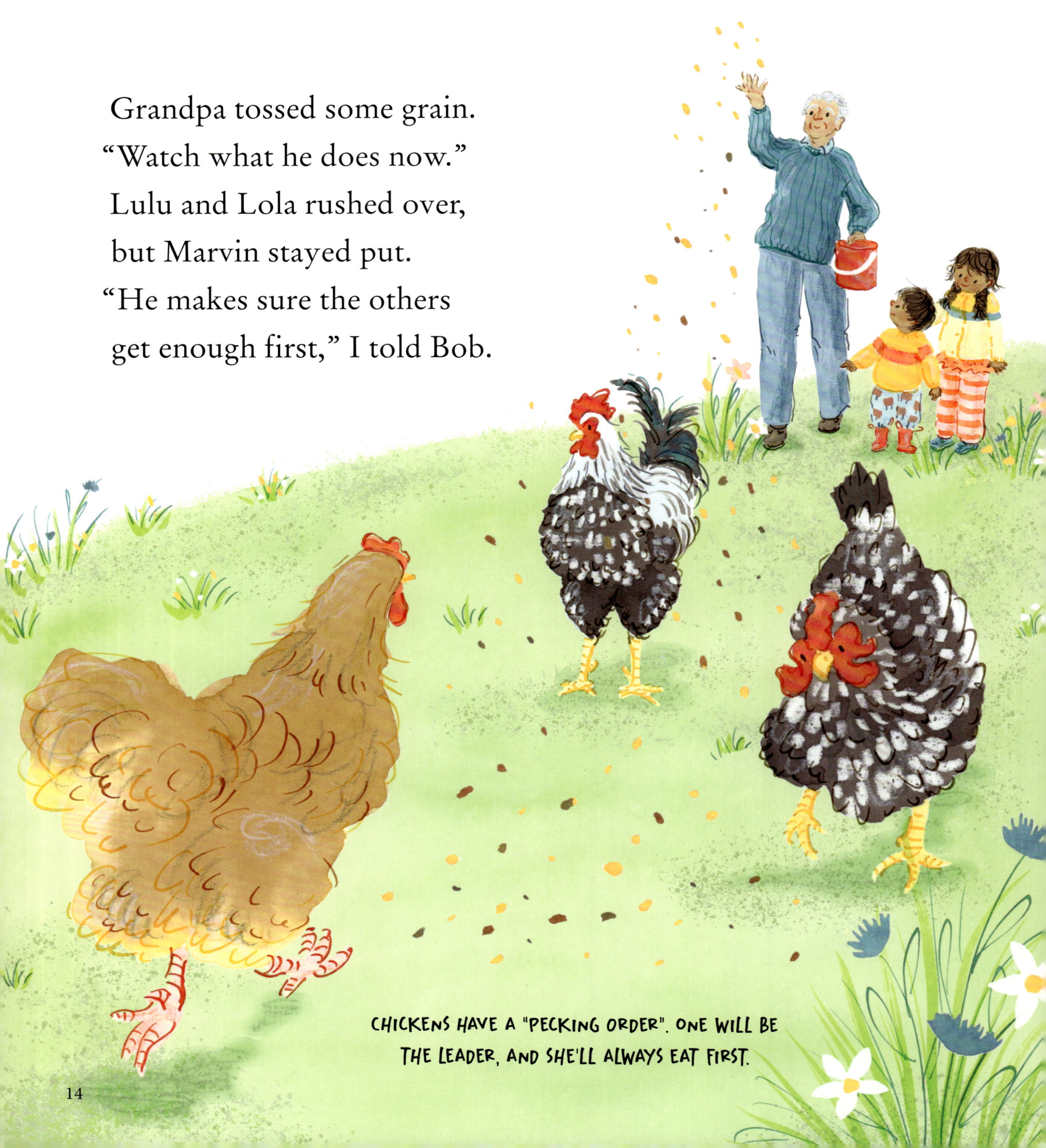

CHICKENS HAVE A "PECKING ORDER". ONE WILL BE
THE LEADER, AND SHE'LL ALWAYS EAT FIRST.

Sure enough, a couple of minutes later, Marvin started pecking at the grain.

WHEN A ROOSTER IS COURTING
A CHICKEN, HE DANCES!
HE'LL HOP FROM FOOT TO FOOT,
AND PICK UP A DELICIOUS
BIT OF FOOD, THEN DROP IT —
AND PICK IT UP AGAIN.
THIS IS CALLED "TIDBITTING".

"Do you have other chickens?"
Bob wanted to know. I nodded.
"There's a grey and white speckly
one called Lottie. She's different
from the others… There are
hundreds of different
kinds of chickens."

THERE ARE SOMEWHERE AROUND 300
SPECIES OF CHICKENS IN THE WORLD.

"Bob, would you like to meet
Lottie?" asked Grandpa.
"She's doing something exciting!
But you have to keep quiet.
We mustn't disturb her."

Grandpa opened the nest box … and there was Lottie.
"She's sitting on her eggs," he said. "Listen!"
Lottie was clucking softly, as if she was
whispering in chicken language.

THE MOTHER DOESN'T START SITTING ON THE EGGS UNTIL SHE'S LAID THE
LAST ONE … OTHERWISE, THEY'D ALL HATCH AT DIFFERENT TIMES.

"What's she saying?" Bob asked.
"'Come on out, little chicks!
Bob and Julie want to meet
you!'" said Grandpa, chuckling.

ONLY EGGS THAT HAVE BEEN "FERTILIZED"
(WHERE A CHICKEN HAS MATED WITH A
ROOSTER) HATCH INTO CHICKENS. THE EGGS
THAT ARE SOLD IN SHOPS AREN'T FERTILIZED.

The eggs didn't hatch all day – but the next morning, we hurried to the hen house. There was Lottie …

and beside her was an egg with a tiny hole.

"Watch!" Grandpa said. We held our breath as the hole became a crack …

and then, the top of the egg pushed up like a lid.

"There she is," whispered Grandpa.

CHICKS HAVE A TINY "EGG TOOTH" TO HELP THEM BREAK THE SHELL, LIKE A TEENY RHINO HORN. IT FALLS OFF SOON AFTER THEY'VE HATCHED.

It was nearly lunchtime before the chick finally crawled out of the shell. She wasn't how we expected, she was all wet and straggly! Soon, she had crept under her mum's soft fluffy bottom.

Before long, three more eggs
had little holes in them!
"Where's our chick gone?"
Bob asked and, very gently,
Grandpa lifted up Lottie.

There was our chick – now
a beautiful, fluffy yellow.

THE YELLOW COMES
FROM THE YELLOW
"YOLK" AT THE CENTRE
OF THE EGG.

NOT ALL CHICKS ARE YELLOW:
JERSEY GIANT CHICKS ARE
BLACK AND WHITE, AND
RHODE ISLAND RED CHICKS
ARE GOLD AND BROWN.

When Mum came to take us home,
Bob told her, "I LOVE chickens!"
"Me too," I said.

Grandpa laughed.
"And I love YOU,
my little chicks!"

## AUTHOR'S NOTE

Chickens make wonderful pets!
But you need to look after them
properly – and make sure they have
plenty of space to roam. They need
food and water every day, and to be
shut up safely at night.

Silkies or Cochin chickens are easy
to tame and, when a Cochin decides
you're her friend, she'll follow you
round! And Orpingtons, like Lola, are
gentle birds and often love a cuddle.

## INDEX

## MORE INFORMATION

If you'd like to find out more about chickens, and how to take care of them, a good book to read next might be *Chickenology: The Ultimate Encyclopedia* by Barbara Sandri and Francesco Giubbilini, illustrated by Camilla Pintonato (Princeton Architectural Press, 2021).